KU-798-619

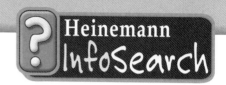
Heinemann InfoSearch

Earth's Precious Resources

Rocks
A resource our world depends on

Heinemann
LIBRARY

Ian Graham

www.heinemann.co.uk/library

Visit our website to find out more information about **Heinemann Library** books.

To order:
☎ Phone 44 (0) 1865 888066
📄 Send a fax to 44 (0) 1865 314091
💻 Visit the Heinemann Bookshop at www.heinemann.co.uk/library to browse our catalogue and order online.

First published in Great Britain by Heinemann Library, Halley Court, Jordan Hill, Oxford OX2 8EJ, part of Harcourt Education.
Heinemann is a registered trademark of Harcourt Education Ltd.

Editorial: Andrew Farrow and Dan Nunn
Design: David Poole and Paul Myerscough
Picture Research: Melissa Allison and Andrea Sadler
Production: Duncan Gilbert

Originated by Ambassador Litho Ltd
Printed in China by WKT Company Limited

ISBN 0 431 11553 2
08 07 06 05 04
10 9 8 7 6 5 4 3 2 1

British Library Cataloguing in Publication Data

Graham, Ian
Rocks: a resource our world depends on. – (Earth's precious resources)
1. Rocks – Juvenile literature 2. Stone industry and trade – Juvenile literature
I. Title
552
A full catalogue record for this book is available from the British Library.

Acknowledgements

The publishers would like to thank the following for permission to reproduce photographs: Bridgeman Art Library p. **18**; Construction Photography p. **8**; Corbis pp. **13**, **22** (Barnabas Bosshart), **23** (Charles E. Rotkin), **25** (Bettmann), **29**; Ecoscene pp. **16** (Peter Hulme), **28 top** (Anthony Cooper), **28 bottom** (Tony Hamblin FRPS); FLPA pp. **5 top** (Maurice Nimmo), **5 bottom** (Maurice Nimmo), **14** (David Hosking); Getty Images/Photodisc pp. **7**, **9**, **19 bottom**; Harcourt Education Ltd p. **4** (Dave Johnson), **6** (Peter Evans), **10** (Visual Image); NOAA pp. **12**, **24 top**, **24 bottom**, **26**, **27**; QA Photos pp. **15**, **19 top**, **21**; Science Photo Library pp. **17** (Publiphoto Diffusion/A. Comu), **20 bottom** (NASA); Topham Picturepoint p. **20 top** (ImageWorks).

Cover photograph reproduced with permission of Corbis/Hans Georg Roth.

Every effort has been made to contact copyright holders of any material reproduced in this book. Any omissions will be rectified in subsequent printings if notice is given to the publishers.

The paper used to print this book comes from sustainable resources.

Contents

Any words appearing in the text in bold, **like this**, are explained in the Glossary.

What is rock?

Rock is a natural resource found in the ground. There are different types of rock. Some are light, some are heavy, while some are harder than others. They are often different colours, because they contain different mixtures of **minerals**. Minerals are made from tiny crystals. These are like grains of salt, joined together.

There are three main types of rock – igneous, sedimentary and metamorphic. They are different because they are formed in different ways.

Igneous rock

Igneous rock is made when hot, liquid rock, called **magma** or **lava**, cools down and becomes solid. Igneous means fiery. Basalt and **granite** are examples of igneous rock.

This is granite, an igneous rock. You can see the crystals of different minerals that make up the rock.

Sedimentary rock

Frost, wind, the Sun's heat and other forces of nature break down rock into smaller and smaller pieces. Eventually they are as small as grains of **sand**. Rain washes them into rivers and the sea, where they sink to the bottom. In this form they are known as sediment. The weight of more and more material piling up on top of them presses the **particles** together so tightly that they form rock. Sandstone is one example of sedimentary rock.

Sandstone is a sedimentary rock. You can see the grains of sand and other particles that have been pressed together to make the rock.

Metamorphic rock

Rock is sometimes heated or squashed so much that it changes into a new type of rock, called metamorphic rock. Metamorphic just means changed. **Marble** is one example of metamorphic rock. It starts as a chalky sedimentary rock called **limestone**. Then heat from hot rock underground and the weight of earth and water above pressing down change it into marble.

Marble is a metamorphic rock. It usually contains coloured swirls and veins made from different minerals.

What is rock used for?

You can see rock all around you. It is in your home and your streets. Some types of rock are very hard and long-lasting. This makes rock ideal as a building material. When rock is taken from nature and used for a purpose, such as building, it is called stone. Thousands of years ago, ancient peoples made their most important buildings from stone. Some of them still exist today, because they were made from this hard, long-lasting material. The Great Pyramid of Khufu at Giza, in Egypt, was built 4500 years ago. It contains 2.3 **million** massive stones. Stone was chosen as the best material to protect the pharaoh (Egyptian king) buried inside it for the rest of time.

It took thousands of people twenty years to build Egypt's Great Pyramid.

Did you know?

When the pyramids at Giza, in Egypt, were built, they were covered with smooth, white **limestone**. Most of the limestone is now gone. It either fell away or was stolen and used in other buildings.

How is rock used for building today?

Today, crushed rock is used in the foundations, the deepest layers, of roads and buildings. More expensive types of stone, such as **marble**, are sometimes used to make the walls of grand buildings.

Why do people go to mountains?

Mountains are giant piles of rock that tower over the surrounding land. Today, tourists visit mountains to look at them and photograph them. Mountaineers climb them. In ancient times, people were attracted to mountains for different reasons. Some people worshipped them as gods. Others thought that gods lived on their snow-capped, cloud-covered tops.

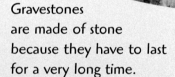

Gravestones are made of stone because they have to last for a very long time.

Did you know?

The ancient Greek people believed that Mount Olympus was the home of the gods. The Maori people of New Zealand call the country's tallest mountain Aoraki. In their legends, Aoraki was a son of the Sky Father, Raki, turned to rock.

How is rock used to clean things?

Some cleaning products contain fine powdered rock. When it is rubbed over something, the rough **particles** wear away dirt and grime on the surface. One way of cleaning stone buildings, called **sand**-blasting, makes use of rock particles too. Grains of sand, or a similar material, are blown down a hose by a jet of air. They fly out and hit the stone. They act like millions of tiny hammers, beating away all of the dirt and cleaning the stone.

How is rock used in sport?

Heavy stones were used for weightlifting competitions in the past. Today, the sport of curling still uses stones. Two teams slide heavy stones along ice, so that the stones stop as close as possible to a target, called the tee or button.

Dirt, grime and soot that has built up on stone buildings over many years can be cleaned off by sand–blasting.

CASE STUDY:
Mount Rushmore, USA

One of the biggest and most impressive **monuments** made from rock anywhere in the world is Mount Rushmore National **Memorial** in the USA. It is a **sculpture** of four heads, about 18 metres (60 feet) high, in the side of a mountain! They are the heads of four US presidents – George Washington, Thomas Jefferson, Theodore Roosevelt and Abraham Lincoln. Explosives were used to blast half a **million** tonnes of rock away. Then workers hanging from cables used hammers and drills to carve away the rest of the rock. The **granite** rock was so hard that the drills had to be re-sharpened after only 45 centimetres (18 inches) of drilling. The work began in 1927 and finished in 1941.

The four heads of the Mount Rushmore National Memorial are carved out of a mountain.

Where is rock found?

Rock is found all over the Earth and also inside it. The surface of the Earth is made from rock. In many places, it is covered with soil or water, but if you dig down far enough, you will reach rock. The Earth is not solid rock all the way through. The rock at the surface is called the **crust**. Underneath the crust, there is a layer about 2900 kilometres (1810 miles) deep, called the mantle. The rock the mantle is made from, called **magma**, is so hot that it flows slowly, like thick treacle. At the centre of the Earth, there is a ball-shaped **core** about 7000 kilometres (4350 miles) across. It is made mainly from iron. The centre of the core is solid, but the outside part is liquid.

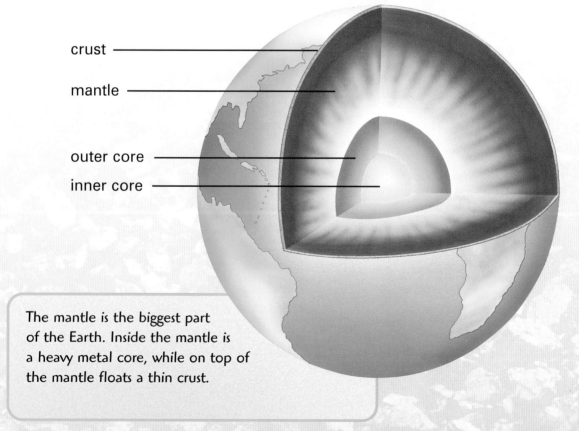

crust

mantle

outer core

inner core

The mantle is the biggest part of the Earth. Inside the mantle is a heavy metal core, while on top of the mantle floats a thin crust.

What is the Earth's crust like?

The Earth's crust is not a solid shell of rock. It is made up of pieces, called plates, like a cracked egg shell. The plates move slowly in different directions. In places where they push against each other, there are **earthquakes** and **volcanoes**. Underneath the oceans, some plates are moving apart. Molten (melted) rock rises up into the gap between them and cools to form solid rock.

How thick is the Earth's crust?

The Earth's crust is thinnest under the middle of the oceans. Here, it is as little as 6 kilometres (4 miles) thick. The rest of the crust is much thicker, up to about 70 kilometres (44 miles) thick. It is thickest underneath the land.

The Earth's crust is divided into plates of rock.

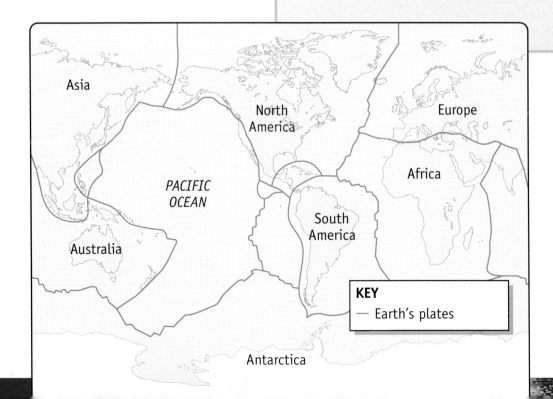

Asia

North America

Europe

PACIFIC OCEAN

Africa

South America

Australia

KEY
— Earth's plates

Antarctica

How does the Earth's crust move?

The smoke from a fire floats upwards, because hot air rises. Very hot rock inside the Earth rises too, but much more slowly. Heat from the centre of the Earth makes magma rise up through the mantle. As the magma rises, it cools and sinks down again. These slow-moving currents in the mantle make the crust on top of it move too.

The forces that move the Earth's crust are enormous. They are strong enough to bend or break the rocky crust. If the rock is hot enough and pushed slowly enough, it folds like treacle. If the rock is colder and more brittle, and pushed too quickly, it breaks. A break in the Earth's crust is called a fault.

Did you know?

The oldest of the Earth's rocks found so far are 4 **billion** years old. They were found in Canada.

The San Andreas fault, where two of the world's great crust plates meet, runs right through the US state of California.

CASE STUDY:
Mount Everest

The tallest mountain on Earth is Mount Everest. It is located in the Himalayan mountain range on the border between Nepal and China. Its summit (highest point) stands 8850 metres (29,035 feet) above sea level. It was climbed for the first time in 1953, when two climbers named Edmund Hilary and Tenzing Norgay stepped onto its summit.

The Himalayas lie along the line where two plates of the Earth's **crust** meet. The plate with India on top is pushing northwards into the plate that Europe and Asia sit on. They met 50 **million** years ago. As one plate pushed into the other, the ground was forced upwards to form the mountains. About half a million years ago, they became the tallest mountains on Earth.

Mount Everest was found to be the tallest mountain on Earth in 1852.

CASE STUDY:
Uluru (Ayer's Rock), Australia

Uluru is one of the most famous pieces of rock on Earth. It used to be known as Ayer's Rock. It rises to a height of 335 metres (1100 feet) above the surrounding desert in Australia's Northern Territory. It measures 3.6 kilometres (2.25 miles) long by 2 kilometres (1.25 miles) wide. Although it looks huge, it is just the tip of a mountain that stood on an ocean floor 500 **million** years ago. Then movements in the Earth's **crust** pushed the ocean floor upwards. Today, Uluru's base is buried nearly 6 kilometres (4 miles) below the ground and only the very top can be seen. It is a sacred place for Aborigines, Australia's native people, who believe it is home to spirits of beings from their history.

Uluru in Australia appears to turn a deep orange-red colour in the morning and evening, when the Sun is low in the sky. Uluru is made of rock called arkose, which is a type of sandstone.

How is rock processed?

Rock is processed in many different ways. It may simply be washed before it is used. If the pieces are too big, they are crushed and sorted into different sizes. Rock can be heated and mixed with other materials to extract (take out) metals, such as iron. **Limestone** is used to make cement and cement is used to make concrete.

What is concrete?

Concrete is a mixture of **sand**, cement, water and small pieces of rock called gravel. Concrete can be poured and shaped when it is freshly mixed. It then sets as hard as rock.

Did you know?

The ancient Romans made cement more than 2000 years ago. It is also known as pozzolana because it contained volcanic ash found near the town of Pozzuoli.

This vehicle was used to crush rock during the construction of the Channel Tunnel between England and France.

Why are some rocks called ores?

Rocks are made from thousands of different **minerals**. About 100 of these minerals contain useful materials, mainly metals. These minerals are called ore minerals, or **ores**. Small amounts of pure metals – such as gold, copper and tin – are found in the ground, but most metals have to be extracted from ores. Iron comes from several different ores, including haematite and magnetite. Tin comes from an ore called cassiterite.

How do we get metal from rock?

In nature, ores are usually mixed together with other types of rock in the ground. Each ore has to be separated from the unwanted rock.

Rock is dug out of the ground at places called **quarries**.

Then the metal is extracted from the ore. This is done by a process called smelting. Smelting works by heating the ore inside a furnace to such a high temperature that the metal melts and runs out. As it cools, it changes from a liquid into solid metal.

How hot does a furnace have to be?

Different metals melt at different temperatures. A furnace has to be hot enough to melt the metal, so the temperature of a furnace depends on which metal it produces. Copper melts at 1083 °C (1981 °F) but iron does not melt until it reaches a temperature of 1535 °C (2795 °F).

Metals are produced by smelting ores in furnaces.

Did you know?

The first metal that people obtained by smelting was copper, about 7000 years ago.

How long have people used rock?

People have made things from rock, by hammering it or cutting it, for more than two **million** years. **Stone Age** people made axes and other tools out of rock. Ancient people also carved and painted rock. We know a lot about ancient Egypt because many of its stone buildings and **monuments** are covered with paintings and carvings that tell stories of its people and their history. Today, stone statues and other **sculptures** in public places mark important events and people in our history.

What did prehistoric people use flint for?

Stone Age people used all sorts of rock, but rock called flint was especially useful. When a piece of flint was hit in the right way, razor-sharp flakes flew off it. These flakes made excellent cutting tools.

This beautiful statue of David was made from a block of **marble** 500 years ago by the Italian artist Michelangelo.

How do scientists use rocks?

Scientists who study rocks are called **geologists**. Geologists use rocks to learn more about the Earth and what has happened to it since it formed about 4.6 **billion** years ago. They also study rocks to find valuable materials such as oil, gold and other metals. Rocks contain a record of the history of the Earth and the plants and animals that have lived on it.

Geologists collect rock samples and take them back to their laboratory to study.

How do rocks record life on Earth?

When animals that lived **millions** of years ago died, their soft parts rotted away quickly, leaving bones, teeth and shells. If they died in water, they were soon covered with mud. In time, water rich in **minerals** soaked through the bones and changed them into **fossils**.

Some rocks contain fossils, the remains of long-dead plants and animals.

What have we learned about the Moon by studying rocks?

Twelve US astronauts who landed on the Moon brought 380 kilogrammes (840 pounds) of moon-rocks back to Earth with them. By studying these rocks, scientists have learned more about how the Moon was formed. Scientists believe the Earth was hit by a large object the size of a planet like Mars. It blasted rock out of the Earth's surface into space. All the millions of pieces of rock slowly clumped together to form the Moon. Unmanned spacecraft are still being sent to the Moon and the planets to study them.

The Mars Pathfinder space mission landed the Sojourner rover vehicle on the surface of the planet Mars in 1997. It moved around and studied rocks lying on Mars' surface.

Do scientists study other space rocks?

When the Sun and planets formed, lots of pieces of rock were left over. Many of them are still flying through space today. A few hit the Earth every year. They are called meteorites. Geologists collect meteorites and study them.

Meteorites are rocks from space that land on Earth.

CASE STUDY:
The Channel Tunnel

In 1994, the Channel Tunnel opened after almost seven years of work. The tunnel lies under the sea between England and France. Before tunnelling could begin, **geologists** had to find out what sort of rock lay beneath the seabed. They found several different layers of rock. One layer was chalk marl, which is a mixture of chalk and a type of soil called clay. It is a soft rock and also waterproof, making it ideal for digging tunnels under the sea.

Giant machines tunnelled through the rock. Each machine wedged itself in the tunnel and cutters on the front carved away the rock. Then the whole machine was pushed forwards to cut more rock away. They cut through as much as 75 metres (245 feet) of rock every day.

Tunnel-boring machines dug all the way from England to France underneath the English Channel.

How is rock moved around?

Rock is hard to move, because of its great weight. Trucks haul rock out of **quarries** and **mines**. Trains and ships transport it over greater distances. The ships are called bulk carriers. Special bulk carriers called **ore** carriers are used for the heaviest loads. About 5000 bulk carrier ships carry **cargoes** such as iron ore around the world. The biggest ore carriers can each transport up to 300,000 tonnes of ore.

Rock and ore are transported long distances by ship and trains. This train is transporting iron ore.

How did people move rock without modern machines?

People in the ancient world moved very big blocks of rock without the powerful machines we have today. About 5000 years ago in England, people began to build a **monument** called Stonehenge. Over the next 1000 years, circles of giant stones were added to it. The first 80 stones weighed up to 4 tonnes each.

Then, 30 more stones weighing up to 50 tonnes each were added – that's the same weight as about 30 cars! The stones were moved on water using wooden rafts whenever possible. On land, they were probably dragged on sleds or pushed along on top of logs. The logs acted as rollers, making it easier to move the stones.

How is rock transported by road today?

The trucks used to transport rock in quarries and mines are giant vehicles. They are far too big to travel on ordinary roads. Rock is transported by road in tipper trucks. These trucks have a cargo tank at the back that can be tipped up. When the front end of the tank is raised, the back opens and the load slides out onto the ground.

Giant machines dig rock out of the ground. The rock is then loaded into tipper trucks like this one.

How can rock be dangerous?

Rock is dangerous when it falls or flies through the air, because it is so heavy. Falling rocks can block roads and hurt climbers. Rock-falls in **mines** can block tunnels and trap miners. **Volcanoes** can throw out enough rock and ash to bury a whole town. **Earthquakes** crack the ground open and cause dangerous rockslides.

Rockslides can block roads and bury buildings.

Radiation

Rock can be dangerous because of what it contains. Some substances give out harmful **particles** or rays, called radiation. Rocks that contain uranium give out a gas called radon and radon gives out radiation. The gas can collect in houses built on top of the rock. Breathing in too much radon for a long time can harm people's health. Houses at risk are often fitted with air pumps to blow the gas away.

Did you know?

There are about twenty serious earthquakes every year. Some earthquakes are powerful enough to make buildings collapse.

CASE STUDY:
The Vaiont Dam landslide, Italy

One of the biggest dams in the world was built across the Vaiont River in Italy in 1961. In 1963 a giant wall of water swept down the valley below the dam and drowned 2500 people. Experts thought the dam must have burst, but they were amazed to see that it was still there!

The rock on each side of the valley had a layer of clay running through it. The water behind the dam stopped water in the valley walls from draining away. The water made the clay so slippery that the rock above it slid off. **Millions** of tonnes of rock fell into the **reservoir**, throwing up a giant wave. The wave then spilled over the top of the dam into the valley below.

The Vaiont Dam disaster was caused by a huge rockslide.

Why are volcanoes dangerous?

When a **volcano** erupts, it throws out rock so hot that it has melted and turned into a liquid. This liquid rock is called **lava**. When the red-hot lava cools, it turns into a type of rock called basalt. Volcanoes can erupt in different ways. Sometimes, lava pours out and flows down the sides of a volcano, like a river of fire. Sometimes, the lava explodes out of a volcano with enormous force, hurling huge rocks high into the air.

Volcanoes that erupt are called active volcanoes. Volcanoes that have not erupted for a long time are called dormant.

Did you know?

There are about 500 active volcanoes in the world today.

Volcanoes can erupt with a fiery explosion of red-hot lava. This is Kilauea Volcano, in Hawaii.

CASE STUDY:
Mount St Helens, USA

The biggest rockslide in **recorded history** happened in the USA. A **volcano** called Mount St Helens had not erupted for 123 years. Then, in 1980, the ground shook and a large bulge appeared on one side of the mountain. The bulge was **magma** rising up inside the mountain. On May 18, the whole bulging side of the mountain slid away and the magma underneath it exploded out. The top 400 metres (1312 feet) of the mountain disappeared in just a few seconds. Snow and ice from the mountain-top melted and formed rivers. These raging torrents carried thousands of tonnes of loose rocks down the mountainside. Mount St Helens continued erupting for six years. When all the rocks came to rest and the **lava** cooled, the mountain and the land all around it had changed forever.

In 1980 the US volcano Mount St Helens erupted. The magma that poured out flattened forests, killed 57 people and thousands of animals, and damaged 27 bridges and nearly 200 homes.

What about the environment?

Digging rock out of the ground creates ugly scars in the land and damages natural **habitats**. Rock is usually hauled away in big trucks. The noise, dust and heavy traffic can be a nuisance to people living nearby. When a **quarry** or a **mine** closes, the site is often left to return to nature by itself. Sometimes, people try to speed this up by covering the ground with new soil and plants. This is called landscaping.

Although closed quarries or mines can look natural again after they have been landscaped, it still takes nature many years to fully recover.

Digging up limestone

The **limestone** pavement is a rare type of rock formation that can be up to 300 **million** years old. Some limestone pavements have been destroyed to supply rock for gardens.

Limestone pavements like this have been destroyed by quarrying.

Will rock ever run out?

We will never run out of rock. New rock is constantly being formed by natural processes in the Earth. **Volcanoes** bring new rock up to the surface all the time.

Using stone again

In ancient times, people often took materials from old buildings and walls and used them for new buildings. When a wall collapsed or a building was left empty, the stones it was built from were carried away and used again. This still happens today. When old buildings are knocked down, the materials are sorted into bricks, stone blocks, roof tiles, wooden beams, flooring and so on, so that they can be used again.

The Hawaiian islands, in the Pacific Ocean, are the tips of volcanoes. As more volcanoes erupt, more new land will be formed.

Glossary

billion huge number, equal to one thousand million

cargo goods or materials transported in a vehicle, especially in large amounts

core central section

crust rock that forms the surface of the Earth

earthquake sudden, violent movement of the Earth

fossils remains of long-dead plants and animals

geologist someone who studies geology, the science of rocks

granite type of igneous rock that is grey and very hard. It is commonly used in building.

habitat natural home of plants and animals

lava rock produced by volcanoes, so hot that it is liquid

limestone chalky sedimentary rock

magma part-liquid, part-solid rock in the mantle, the layer underneath the Earth's crust

marble type of metamorphic rock. It usually contains coloured swirls and veins made from different minerals.

memorial another word for a monument

million very big number, equal to one thousand thousands

mine hole dug in the ground so that mineral ores or coal can be taken out. People who work in mines are called miners, and the digging they do is called mining.

minerals materials that rocks are made of. Most minerals are made up from two or more substances combined.

monument statue, building, gravestone or other object that is created to honour the memory of someone or something

ore mineral from which a metal, or metals, can be extracted (taken out)

particle tiny piece

quarry hole dug in the ground to remove stone, gravel or sand

recorded history the time since people started writing things down – more than 5000 years ago

reservoir human-made lake

sand particles of rock less than 2 millimetres across. Most sand is made from particles of a mineral called quartz, from rock that was worn down by the weather.

sculpture work of art made by carving stone or wood, or by pouring liquid metal or plastic into a mould

Stone Age time in human history when people made tools from stone. It started about 700,000 years ago. It lasted until about 4000–5000 years ago.

volcano hole in the Earth's crust where lava comes out. The lava often builds up to form a mountain.

Find out more

Books

Collins Wild Guide: Rocks and Minerals, Adrian Jones (Collins, 2000)

DK Eyewitness Books: Rocks and Minerals, R. F. Symes (Dorling Kindersley, 2003)

Philip's Minerals: Rocks and Fossils, W. R. Hamilton, A. R. Woolley and A. C. Bishop (Philip's, 2001)

Usborne Spotter's Guides: Rocks and Minerals, A. R. Woolley (Usborne Publishing, 2000)

Websites

www.idahoptv.org/dialogue4kids/season3/rocks/facts.html
Information about rocks and minerals from Idaho Public Television.

www.geology.usgs.gov/ask-a-geo.html
A website for asking a geologist questions.

www.earthquake.usgs.gov/faq/plates.html
Answers to questions about the Earth's crust and earthquakes from the US Geological Survey.

media.graniteschools.org/Curriculum/mt_rush/construc.htm
The story of how the Mount Rushmore sculpture was made.

Disclaimer

All the Internet addresses (URLs) given in this book were valid at the time of going to press. However, due to the dynamic nature of the Internet, some addresses may have changed, or sites may have ceased to exist since publication. While the author and publishers regret any inconvenience this may cause readers, no responsibility for any such changes can be accepted by either the author or the publishers.

Index

Titles in the *Earth's Precious Resources* series include:

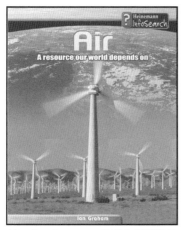

Hardback   0 431 11556 7

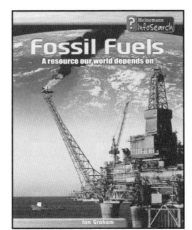

Hardback   0 431 11550 8

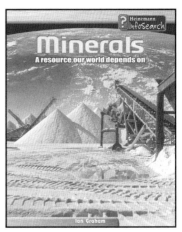

Hardback   0 431 11552 4

Hardback   0 431 11551 6

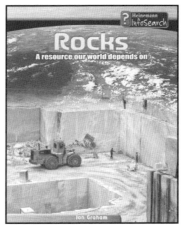

Hardback   0 431 11553 2

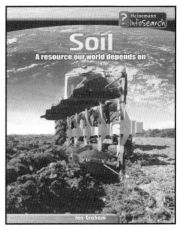

Hardback   0 431 11554 0

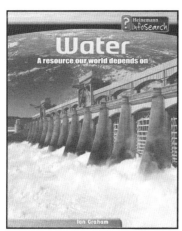

Hardback   0 431 11555 9

Find out about the other titles in this series on our website www.heinemann.co.uk/library